MW01193199

Notebook

To

Happy Birthday!

With love and best wishes from:

Image credits: Imperial War Museum, National Archives UK, Sicnag, Micha Perry/National Photo Library of Israel, JT Brown, National Archives and Record Administration.
© Montpelier Publishing, London 2017

1948 Birthday Notebook

1 January
The LMS, LNER, GWR and SR railway companies are
nationalised to form British Railways.

1948 Birthday Notebook

1 January
Italy's new Republican constitution comes into effect.

_____

_____

_____

_____

_____

_____

_____

_____

_____

_____

_____

_____

_____

_____

1948 Birthday Notebook

4 January
Burma granted independence from Britain with Sao Shwe Thaik as President.

_____

_____

_____

_____

_____

_____

_____

_____

_____

_____

_____

_____

_____

_____

_____

_____

1948 Birthday Notebook

12 January
Mahatma Gandhi goes on hunger strike in protest against sectarian violence following end of British rule in India.

_____

_____

_____

_____

_____

_____

_____

_____

_____

_____

_____

_____

_____

_____

1948 Birthday Notebook

12 January
The Co-Operative Society (Co-Op) opens its first
supermarket, at Manor Park, London.

_____

_____

_____

_____

_____

_____

_____

_____

_____

_____

_____

_____

_____

_____

◇◇◇

17 January
Highest ever attendance at an English football league game
as 83,260 people attend Manchester United *v* Arsenal.

_____

_____

_____

_____

_____

_____

_____

_____

_____

_____

_____

_____

_____

23 January
Mañana (Is Soon Enough for Me) by Peggy Lee enters the charts and remains there for 21 weeks, nine of them at Number One.

1948 Birthday Notebook

30 January
Gandhi assassinated in New Delhi by Nathuram Godse.

◇◇◇

30 January
Flying pioneer Orville Wright dies aged 76.

◇◇◇

31 January
The British crown colony of the Malayan Union, Penang and Malacca form the Federation of Malaya.

_____

_____

_____

_____

_____

_____

_____

_____

_____

_____

_____

_____

_____

1948 Birthday Notebook

4 February
Ceylon (later known as Sri Lanka) becomes independent from Britain.

_____

_____

_____

_____

_____

_____

_____

_____

_____

_____

_____

_____

_____

_____

1948 Birthday Notebook

16 February
Miranda, innermost of the large moons of Uranus, is
discovered by Gerard Kuiper.

1948 Birthday Notebook

◇◇

18 February
Éamon de Valera, Irish head of government since 1932, loses
power to an opposition coalition.

_____

_____

_____

_____

_____

_____

_____

_____

_____

_____

_____

_____

_____

◇◇

21 February
The United States stock car racing organization NASCAR is
founded by Bill France, Sr.

_____

_____

_____

_____

_____

_____

_____

_____

_____

_____

_____

_____

_____

25 February
Communists seize power in Czechoslovakia.

1948 Birthday Notebook

17 March
Britain, France and the Benelux countries sign the Treaty of
Brussels, the forerunner of NATO.

_____

_____

_____

_____

_____

_____

_____

_____

_____

_____

_____

_____

_____

_____

1948 Birthday Notebook

17 March
Hell's Angels motorcycle club founded in California.

_____

_____

_____

_____

_____

_____

_____

_____

_____

_____

_____

_____

_____

_____

1948 Birthday Notebook

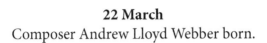

22 March
Composer Andrew Lloyd Webber born.

_____

_____

_____

_____

_____

_____

_____

_____

_____

_____

_____

_____

_____

_____

_____

◇◇

28 March
Jazz musician Nat King Cole marries Maria Hawkins in New York.

_____

_____

_____

_____

_____

_____

_____

_____

_____

_____

_____

_____

_____

_____

1 April
Electricity supply in the UK is nationalised; gas supplies are nationalised later in the year.

_____

_____

_____

_____

_____

_____

_____

_____

_____

_____

_____

_____

_____

_____

1948 Birthday Notebook

3 April
US President Harry S. Truman signs the Marshall Plan,
which authorizes $5 billion in aid for 16 countries.

_____

_____

_____

_____

_____

_____

_____

_____

_____

_____

_____

_____

_____

_____

1948 Birthday Notebook

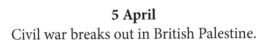

5 April
Civil war breaks out in British Palestine.

_____

_____

_____

_____

_____

_____

_____

_____

_____

_____

_____

_____

_____

_____

◇◇◇

7 April
The World Health Organisation founded.

1948 Birthday Notebook

13 May
The National Assistance Act for social welfare in the UK
replaces the Poor Law system, dating from the 19th century.

_____

_____

_____

_____

_____

_____

_____

_____

_____

_____

_____

_____

_____

_____

_____

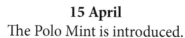

15 April
The Polo Mint is introduced.

_____

_____

_____

_____

_____

_____

_____

_____

_____

_____

_____

_____

_____

_____

◇◇

19 April
ABC Television begins broadcasting in the USA.

_____

_____

_____

_____

_____

_____

_____

_____

_____

_____

_____

_____

_____

_____

1948 Birthday Notebook

30 April
The Land Rover is launched at the Amsterdam Motor Show.

1948 Birthday Notebook

4 May
The film version of Shakespeare's *Hamlet*, starring Laurence Olivier, premieres in London.

14 May
Israel declares itself an independent state as British rule in
the region ends.

_____

_____

_____

_____

_____

_____

_____

_____

_____

_____

_____

_____

_____

_____

_____

28 May
Apartheid begins in South Africa following election of the
National Party.

1948 Birthday Notebook

◇◇

5-13 June
The first Aldeburgh Festival takes place, under the direction
of musicians Benjamin Britten and Peter Pears.

◇◇◇

11 June

The USA launches its first monkey astronaut, 'Albert', in a V2 rocket to a height of 39 miles.

_____

_____

_____

_____

_____

_____

_____

_____

_____

_____

_____

_____

_____

1948 Birthday Notebook

18 June
A state of emergency is declared in the British colony of
Malaya following a communist uprising.

1948 Birthday Notebook

18 June
The first long play (LP) 33$\frac{1}{3}$ rpm microgroove records are launched by Columbia Records.

_____

_____

_____

_____

_____

_____

_____

_____

_____

_____

_____

_____

_____

◇◇◇

20 June

Toast of the Town (later the *Ed Sullivan Show*) premieres on CBS TV in the USA. It runs until 1971.

_____

_____

_____

_____

_____

_____

_____

_____

_____

_____

_____

_____

_____

_____

1948 Birthday Notebook

22 June
Large-scale immigration to Britain from the West Indies begins with the arrival of the *MV Empire Windrush* at Tilbury.

26 June
The Berlin Airlift begins: supplies are flown to West Berlin
which is cut off by the Soviets.

1948 Birthday Notebook

◇◇◇

1 July
New York's Idlewild Airport (later John F Kennedy Airport)
is opened.

◇◇◇

1 July
The Town and Country Planning Act 1947 comes into force in the UK, introducing planning permission and listed buildings.

◇◇

5 July
The National Health Service (NHS) begins in the UK.

◇◇◇

22 July
The Dominion of Newfoundland votes to join Canada after a referendum.

◇◇◇

25 July
Bread rationing ends in the United Kingdom.

_____

_____

_____

_____

_____

_____

_____

_____

_____

_____

_____

_____

_____

1948 Birthday Notebook

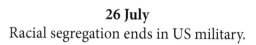

26 July
Racial segregation ends in US military.

1948 Birthday Notebook

29 July
Olympics begin in London; the first held since 1936. They are televised by the BBC using a cable stretched between Wembley and Alexandra Palace.

_____

_____

_____

_____

_____

_____

_____

_____

_____

_____

_____

_____

_____

_____

14 August

1948 Ashes series: Australian victorious as their batsman
Don Bradman plays final game.

16 August
Baseball legend Babe Ruth dies aged 53.

_____

_____

_____

_____

_____

_____

_____

_____

_____

_____

_____

_____

_____

_____

1 September
Judicial corporal punishment (caning with the 'birch')
abolished in the UK.

_____

_____

_____

_____

_____

_____

_____

_____

_____

_____

_____

_____

_____

_____

4 September
Queen Wilhelmina of the Netherlands abdicates on health grounds in favour of Queen Juliana.

_____

_____

_____

_____

_____

_____

_____

_____

_____

_____

_____

_____

_____

_____

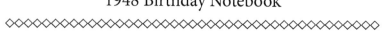
6 September
John Derry becomes the first British pilot to break the sound barrier, flying a De Havilland DH 108.

1948 Birthday Notebook

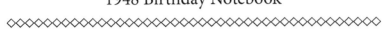

6 September

Powell and Pressburger's ballet film *The Red Shoes* premieres in London, and becomes the top grossing movie of the year.

_____

_____

_____

_____

_____

_____

_____

_____

_____

_____

_____

_____

_____

_____

◇◇

8 September

Terence Rattigan's play *The Browning Version* premieres in London.

9 September
Korea is formally separated into North and South, with Kim Il Sung in power in the North.

_____

_____

_____

_____

_____

_____

_____

_____

_____

_____

_____

_____

_____

_____

◇◇

19 September
Actor Jeremy Irons born.

◇◇

20 September
The Morris Minor is launched at the Earls Court Motor
Show in London. It remains in production until 1971.

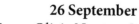

26 September
Singer Olivia Newton-John born.

1948 Birthday Notebook

12 November
International War Crimes Tribunal sentences General Tojo
and 11 other senior Japanese officials to death.

1948 Birthday Notebook

◇◇◇

14 November
HRH Prince Charles, the Prince of Wales born.

1 December
Costa Rica becomes the first country in history to abolish its army, replacing it with a paramilitary police force.

_____

_____

_____

_____

_____

_____

_____

_____

_____

_____

_____

_____

_____

_____

_____

10 December
The United Nations adopts the Universal Declaration of
Human Rights.

_____

_____

_____

_____

_____

_____

_____

_____

_____

_____

_____

_____

_____

_____

CPSIA information can be obtained
at www.ICGtesting.com
Printed in the USA
LVHW03s0827230818
587440LV00001B/7/P

9 781973 904960